LUDLOW PORCH

LONGSTREET PRESS
Atlanta, Georgia

Published by
LONGSTREET PRESS, INC.
A subsidiary of Cox Newspapers,
A division of Cox Enterprises, Inc.
2140 Newmarket Parkway
Suite 118
Marietta, GA 30067

Printed in the United States of America

1st printing 1994

Library of Congress Catalog Card Number: 94-77591

ISBN 1-56352-171-7

This book was printed by Bookcrafters, Fredericksburg,
Virginia.

Film Preparation by Holland Graphics, Inc., Mableton, GA.

Jacket photograph by Warren Bond
Jacket and book design by Laura McDonald

To Denny, Jack, and Phil —
my Three Musketeers

Table of Contents

Introduction

How many times have you heard somebody say, "We're all in this together"? Translated, this means, "Don't worry, if you can't cut it, there will always be somebody to cut it for you."

When all is said and done, we are all in this *alone*. Now, this attitude doesn't mean that we don't all have loving family and friends who are willing to help whenever possible. It simply means when the chips are down, when the day is dark, and the fuse on the dynamite is burning, you must remember this motto: If it is to be, it's up to me.

Tonto summed it up best of all when he turned to the masked rider of the plains and said, "What do you mean 'we,' white man?"

MY
Information
Superhighway

I Just Don't Understand

I have never understood all the fuss about Moon Pies. I fully realize that as a card-carrying, grit-dipping son of these red clay hills, I should love Moon Pies as much as my fellow Southerners. But I've never had one that tasted fresh.

In the Deep South, it is not socially acceptable to turn up your nose at the thought of a Moon Pie snack. In my youth, I would lie about how they tasted—no longer. They taste like pressed sawdust covered with day-old chocolate.

There are fifty million Moon Pies sold every year. Somebody likes them and I don't understand why I don't.

I don't understand why I don't know anybody named Bubba. If we are to believe the media, every third Southern male is named Bubba. Why don't I know any of them?

I don't understand why your druggist will sell you a prescription for hemorrhoids and then tell you to have a nice day.

I don't understand why gas stations lock their bathrooms. What do they think will be stolen? They lock the bathrooms, but they don't lock the cash registers.

I don't understand why the name "John" has fallen into such disrepute. It's a wonderful name. It comes to us from the Bible, yet we show it no respect. We call our toilets "johns"; we refer to the customers of prostitutes as "johns." We even refer to men's underdrawers as "long johns." We call cheap whiskey "who shot John." The letters from girlfriends and wives to soldiers, breaking off the relationship, are called "Dear John" letters. Who was John and what did he do to make so many people mad?

I just don't understand. Why do people up north call soft drinks "sodas"? Soda comes in a box. On the box it says it's good for cleaning, deodorizing, and baking. Soda has absolutely nothing in common with soft drinks. Try washing down a mouthful of peanuts with soda. Try brushing your teeth with a soft drink.

I don't understand where Tarzan got his knife. Or where he kept it.

I don't understand when to say "further" and when to say "farther."

I don't understand why we call liquor stores

"package stores." It seems to me that if you are ashamed of what you sell, you ought not to sell it.

I don't understand why some people say "at this point in time" or "at that point in time." What is wrong with saying "now" and "then"?

I don't understand why somebody will spend two million dollars for a hamburger joint and then put a twenty-dollar speaker at the drive-in window.

I don't understand why old beer cans last forever, but new cars rust out.

I don't understand why the Chinese are such good Ping-Pong players.

I don't understand how the electoral college works or why we need it. Seems to me that the person who gets the most votes ought to get the job.

It seems the more time goes by, the more I don't understand. I wish I were eighteen again, because at eighteen I knew dang near everything there was to know.

It's a Southern Thing

If you have spent any time at all in the American South, you have probably already discovered that we have a very descriptive way of using the language. The best example of this is the way we insult people without sounding mean or vengeful.

The rule for doing this is simple. No matter what you want to say about someone, you simply conclude the sentence by adding these three words: "bless his heart." Once those words pass your lips, you are washed free of all sin. Let me give you a few examples:

"He ain't been worth killing since he got home from the Army. He just lays there all day drinking that old beer and watching the TV while she works her fingers to the bone. He is as sorry as gully dirt and ought to be hung, bless his heart."

"The government ought to take those babies

away from her; she ain't nothin' but a two-bit slut, bless her heart."

"That's the ugliest woman I ever saw. I'd rather kiss a pig's butt than hold her hand, bless her heart."

I reckon it's not what you say, but the way you say it.

Turn Signals

The most frequently heard complaint from northern drivers in the South is "Southern drivers don't use their turn signals." I would be less than honest if I didn't admit that they are right. We don't use our turn signals as much as they do up north, but we have good and valid reasons.

If we live in a small Southern town, we presume that everyone knows where we are going, and turn signals are unnecessary. On the occasions when we venture into Big City traffic, we are afraid that the Big City drivers will see our turn signals and regard them as a sign of weakness. The bottom line is that in the South, we have two basic philosophies on the subject:

1. Yankee drivers use turn signals; Southern drivers pay attention.

2. Real men don't use turn signals; we use hand signals.

The Personals Column

For many years, I was a regular reader of newspaper personals columns. They are usually pretty dull and say things like "Lordy, Lordy, Bill Smith is forty" or "Happy Birthday, Fred."

There are times, however, when they read like a soap opera. I was reading the personals the other day and this one caught my eye:

"I, B. Sidney Whitlock, will not be responsible for the debts of anyone except myself . . . especially that south Georgia white trash by the name of Martha Mae, who tricked me into marrying her while I was so drunk I couldn't tell an apple tree from a 1948 Plymouth."

You just don't overlook an ad like that. A few days later, I noticed this ad:

"B. Sidney Whitlock was not responsible for my debts while I was married to the gravy-sucking pig. He wasn't even responsible for his own debts. As a matter of fact, he ain't never had a dime to his name. He has bad breath, a hammer-toe deformity, and his mama wears a flea collar."

Two days later, the following ad appeared:

"Martha Mae, my Mama is a saint and you ain't fit to slop her hogs. I hope your living bra dies and your tattoo fades. You have brought me nothing but heartaches, and that's what I get for marrying double-wide trailer trash."

Two days later:

"B. Sidney, if your old mama is a saint, then grits ain't groceries. When that ugly dragon finally dies, there ain't gonna be no place for her to go. She is meaner than a snake with a backache. If she didn't stay passed out drunk most of the time, couldn't nobody stand to be in the same county with her. I never particularly cared for her."

Three days later:

"Martha Mae, you got a real mean mouth. April 25, the day we got married, was the blackest day of my life. I hate your guts."

Two days later:

"Sid, you remembered our wedding anniversary. Thanks for the memories. Your little peach, Martha Mae."

Two days later:

"Dear, dear little peach, do you remember the Strangling Frog Motel and the IHOP restaurant on our honeymoon in Callahan, Florida? It was Heaven on Earth. Sid. PS: Mama sends her love."

That was when I stopped reading the personals column. There was just no way this thing was going to turn out all right.

The Word Police

The members of the Word Police are every-where. They are the people who cannot stand it when the English language is abused or misused in any manner. They beat the dashboard of their car when the radio newsman uses the wrong word. They scream at the TV set any-time they hear a mistake.

The Word Police all know when to say "fur-ther" and when to say "farther." They know when to say "who" and when to say "whom." They know the difference between "healthy" and "health-ful."

They did not join the Word Police by choice. They were drafted by Mother Nature and they can't help themselves. My beautiful wife is a high-ranking member of the Word Police. Let's read what she says about her life and times on the force:

I've never considered myself a high-ranking officer of the Word Police—a lowly private perhaps. But aren't we all?

Surely we're all irritated by newscasters who don't bother to look up words for pronunciation. *Melee* isn't "mee'lee," it's "may'lay." *Cuba* isn't "Cue'ba," it's "Coo'ba." Okay, these are just tiny things, you say. Is it tiny when they change a word because they don't like the way it sounds? According to my Oxford English Dictionary, *frigate* is pronounced "frig'it;" there's no other way to pronounce it. "Fri'gate" is not an option. *Uranus* is pronounced "U'rain'us," not "Urine-us." Because third-graders hear "frig it" and "your anus" and giggle, TV decided to change the words. I'm incensed!

Newscasters presumably have people all around them who are paid big bucks to make them look and sound good: writers, directors, producers, and technicians. Why isn't somebody correcting their grammar? I'll tell you one thing, if I hear "extradite *back*" one more time, there's going to be a by-God melee!

I wouldn't want to leave out the sponsors. Every company selling something to eat or drink has declared it "healthy." People and plants are *healthy*. Things that promote good health are *healthful*. I hope those people choke on their tofu.

Television isn't the only culprit. There are many people who don't care about or even pay attention to the language. Like those who say "heigh*th*." They don't say "weigh*th*." I think they're the same ones who say "I feel badly." They don't say "I feel goodly." I wonder why they don't hear the difference.

People don't hear the problem with "hot water heater" either; they just say it. If it's anything, it's a cold water heater. Even the dictionary has given in to "near miss." "Near hit" is certainly more accurate.

Nouns used as verbs and verbs used as nouns are high on my list, too. *Lunch* is what one does at luncheon. *Drape* is what a drapery does.

It's a good thing I'm not an English major. I'd not only be a member of the Word Police, but an obnoxious one!

Stupid People Tricks

Beyond Stupid

About three times a year, the title of my radio show is "Beyond Stupid." The premise is simple, but the results can be surprising as the audience calls in and confesses to doing things that exceed our wildest expectations.

I have come to the conclusion that there are certain times in our lives when two tiny wires in our brain are not touching; when this happens, we are ripe to do something that is truly beyond stupid.

My friend, Paul, had just bought a new boat. It was a honey that slept six, had a nice galley, and was Paul's pride and joy. He spent hours polishing the brass, scrubbing the decks, and making his new toy spotless.

It was time for lunch, and Paul pulled into a beautiful little cove. He walked to the bow of the boat and threw the anchor into the deep, deep water. During his ship-shape chores, he had forgotten to fasten the anchor to a line. He knew as soon as the anchor left his hands that he had done something beyond stupid. There was nothing for him to do except stand there and watch the bubbles rise.

One of my callers admitted to going to the wrong funeral, sitting with strangers, and sobbing for twenty minutes before she realized she should have been across the hall of the large funeral home.

Another caller got into her car, fastened her seat belts, and backed through her closed garage door.

It took me a while to screw up my courage and admit on the air that the previous morning, fresh out of the shower, I had sprayed each armpit with hairspray. I did not realize what I had done until I heard myself screaming as I raised my arms to comb my hair.

One of my favorites was the man who finished brushing his teeth, rinsed his toothbrush carefully, shook out the excess water, and threw the toothbrush in the commode.

Once at home I answered the phone saying, "Go ahead please, you're on the air." The person calling quickly slammed down the phone.

One of my callers admitted to standing in front of a mailbox with a package in one hand and his briefcase in the other. You guessed it . . . he mailed his briefcase.

I don't guess there's anyone in the world who has not tried to take a swig of Budweiser out of a ketchup bottle or poured beer onto his French fries. In most cases, one is too nonplussed to make any comment. There's just nothing to say. There are exceptions, however.

My friend Dan was at a fancy party going through the buffet line. He confused a round butterball with cheese; as his friends watched in horror, he popped the entire butterball in his mouth. Without missing a beat, Dan swallowed, smiled, and said, "Now that's a butterball!"

My friend Tom and his wife were entertaining his boss at a fashionable nightspot. Tom's wife noticed that his fly was open when he returned from the men's room. She whispered the news in his ear when he returned to the table. Trying to be discreet, he zipped up while sitting at the table.

The good news is that nobody noticed the zipping process; the bad news is that he zipped up a piece of the tablecloth in his fly. He asked his boss's wife to dance, stood up, and pulled all of the plates, glasses, and silverware onto the floor.

Sometimes beyond stupid and beyond drunk can be close to the same thing. It was almost

Christmas and a man's wife sent him out to buy a Christmas tree. He used his time out of the house to stop by his favorite pub and toss back a cold one with his buddies. He had seven or eight quick drinks, but even in his drunken haze he knew it was late and that he had to get a tree and get home, or his wife would have his head.

Every Christmas tree lot was closed due to the lateness of the hour. There was only one thing left to do . . . steal a Christmas tree.

When he found a dark, deserted Christmas tree lot, he jumped out of the car, threw a tree in the trunk, slammed the trunk lid, and drove away. He was feeling pretty smug and very proud of his foolproof plan when he was suddenly jerked out of his Christmas reverie by the blue lights of a police car behind him.

He thought, "All I have to do is act sober, and I'll be home free. There is no way they can know I have a stolen Christmas tree in the trunk of my car."

The officer walked up to the car and said, "Sir, have you been drinking?"

The man said, "Of course not, officer."

The policeman said, "Would you mind stepping out of the car?"

When he got out, the cop pointed back down

the road—to the cable coming out of the man's trunk, and the forty Christmas trees that were attached to the cable.

I don't know the end of this story. I can only guess that between the police, the Christmas tree owner, and the wife, the poor fellow did not have a very merry Christmas.

Weight Loss

I don't guess a week goes by that somebody doesn't give me a surefire way to lose weight. They tell me by phone, fax, and face to face. I wouldn't mind so much, but usually the folks who are telling me the best way to lose weight only weigh about eighty pounds and have never had a weight problem a day in their lives.

Let the record clearly show that I know how to lose weight. I don't know how to keep it off, but I know how to lose it. In my life I have lost over 2,000 pounds. That is the equivalent of a very large horse.

I have tried every diet introduced in this country in the last thirty years. I have joined a health spa and Weight Watchers. I have paid a hypnotist named Mandrake Wilson $250.00. I have had some very interesting diets recommended to me, including:

The elephant diet: You can have one elephant a week cooked any way you like it. However, you must personally kill the elephant with a butter knife.

The Brazil diet: You can have one South American a day and all the kumquats you want.

The Alcatraz potato diet: You are locked in a cell, and three times a day a man comes by and shows you a picture of a bowl of mashed potatoes.

The Olympic diet: You are allowed one full meal every four years.

The C.I.A. diet: I understand this is a great diet, but I haven't been able to get anybody to give me the details.

It has been a lifelong battle of the flab with me, and at the present time, the flab is way ahead.

Let Me See If I Have This Straight

I seek, at all times, to be politically correct. I don't tell dumb blonde jokes. I don't laugh at jokes about fat people, bald-headed people, or drunks. I have learned that no matter how much love you have in your heart, it's what comes out of your mouth that counts.

I work hard on a day-to-day basis to make sure that nobody is ever offended by what I say. I must admit, however, that sometimes my ignorance and insensitivity overshadow my good intentions.

A man called me on my radio show one day and started the conversation by saying, "I am a native American." I said, "Me, too." The caller went nuts and proceeded to tell me in a loud voice that I was not and never could be a Native American. Silly me, I had assumed that anyone born here was a native American. Boy was my face red . . . (Oops. I think I did it again.)

I never know what to say when a perfect stranger calls me on the air and starts the conversation by saying, "I'm gay." I don't know how to respond because he just told me something that is none of my business. I generally try to say something nice about Rock Hudson and hope the caller will change the subject.

If I could just figure out the new rules, I could be as politically correct as anybody else. I work on it all the time. So let me see if I've got this straight:

It's racist to sing, play, or enjoy "Dixie," but it is okay for rappers to perform songs that advocate killing police officers and refer to women as "bitches" or "ho's."

The Confederate battle flag is a no-no, but it is okay to fly the flag of folks who brought us Pearl Harbor and the Bataan Death March.

It's okay for Reverend Louis Farrakhan to refer to Jewish people as having a gutter religion, but if a Jew responds in a negative manner, he is racist.

There are many more examples and I find them all confusing. Is it just me, or do the rules keep changing?

From the CRADLE to the GRAVE

The Horrors of Childhood

When we look back on our childhood, we tend to remember it with only the pleasant side of our brain. We only identify the good things in our past. We can instantly recall the wonderful meals prepared by our mothers. We know exactly how her cornbread smelled and tasted. We remember the tire swing that was over the swimming hole. We can harken back to the sound of our father's car as it turned into our yard.

We remember the first high school football game of the season. It was usually on one of the first cool nights of the year. We recall the cute, shapely cheerleaders in their colorful skirts and sweaters, the band members, and the football players.

We remember those first warm days of summer when we were finally allowed by our mothers to go barefooted. In Heaven's great plan, the good, warm, loving memories come to mind more quickly than the bad ones.

In reflecting back on my own childhood, it seems to me that most bad things happened after a grown-up issued one or more of the following statements or questions:

"Go to the board."

I can still remember the chill that went over my little body after my teacher said, "Go to the board." This was not a simple four-word sentence. It came wrapped in a clap of thunder. It echoed around the room, down the hall, and out onto the playground. It meant that everybody in the United States of America was going to be watching me at the blackboard, and no matter what I was asked to write, I wouldn't know how . . . everybody that I respected in the world would know what a dumb ass I really was. In short, my life as a respected member of the fourth grade would be over after I walked those ten paces to the board.

"Did you bring enough for everybody?"

You usually heard this question when the teacher noticed you were chewing gum. It was a dumb question, and was not meant to solicit an answer. It was meant to make you feel like a selfish, cheap little hooligan, and it did.

"This is going on your permanent record."

In the name of God, NOT my permanent record! I didn't even know what it was, but the word "permanent" struck fear in my heart. It did not seem fair that a grade-school teacher could mark me for life.

"If Jerry stuck his head in the oven, would you want to do it, too?"

Mothers gave this answer just after you said, "Jerry's mother lets him."

"Go to the office."

This line was only used by teachers, and it meant you were in serious, serious trouble. I didn't even know what went on in the office, but I did know the stories I had heard from the older boys. I knew about the paddle with a nail in it. I had heard about the whips. I was sure that once I got to the office, "they" (whoever "they" were) could kill me and nobody would even ask what happened to me. I was convinced that the last word on punishment was not the Supreme Court of the United States, it was the office at Central Park School.

"Give me that yo-yo."

I have a theory. I think the Duncan yo-yo

company is completely owned and operated by schoolteachers. I don't think they have a factory at all.

I think when a teacher takes a yo-yo away from a child, she sends it to her home office, and they sell it to a retail outlet, who sells it back to a child, who takes it back to school, and the cycle goes on and on.

You teachers should be ashamed of yourselves! I betcha that if the I.R.S. ever launches a full-scale investigation into America's school-teachers, they will find that many of them are millionaires many times over, from the sale of yo-yos, water pistols, chewing gum, and Boy Scout knives.

"Do you think I am made out of money?"

This was more of an answer than a question, and it not only meant "NO," it meant the discussion was concluded forevermore.

"You look a little peaked."

The *Oxford English Dictionary* defines peaked as "thin, pinched, as from illness or want; sickly looking." When my mother said I looked a little peaked, I didn't know what she meant, but I knew what was next on her list. It was picking the right laxative to make me look "un-peaked."

My sainted mother, and her mother before her, believed there was no malady, sickness, or virus that could withstand ten or twelve bowel movements in a two-hour span.

Once my mother had diagnosed me as peaked, it was necessary that she decide on the proper course of treatment. The laxative could be either a home remedy or something bought over the counter at Glover's Pharmacy. In the South of my childhood, it was common knowledge that doctors had never been able to successfully treat peaked. Medical science was also helpless against "bilious," "stove up," and "out of sorts."

My mother had several laxatives of choice. I hated them all. One of her favorites was called Feen-a-Mint. It was designed to fool children. It looked like Chicklets, a popular chewing gum of the day. Chicklets were pieces of candy-coated chewing gum. Feen-a-Mint was chewing gum coated with a laxative to fool the child into thinking he was getting a treat and not a treatment. I hated it! And to this day, I am unable to even think about chewing gum without having the urge to relieve myself.

My mother also favored a laxative called Ex-lax. I can hear her now, saying, "It tastes just like a Hershey bar." The fact of the matter was it tasted nothing like a Hershey bar. It was bitter and it had no almonds.

Then there was something called Carter's Little Liver Pills. I have never understood how a laxative could be good for your liver, but of course, my mother thought a laxative was good for everything. Carter's Little Liver Pills were smaller that BBs and more powerful than a Sherman tank. I'm convinced that taken in large numbers, Carter's Little Liver Pills could move a loaded pulpwood truck.

So, as we look back over our childhood, let us try to remember that it was not all fun and games like we saw on "The Little Rascals." In the interest of fairness we should also remember that in all probability, nobody on "The Little Rascals" ever looked peaked.

True Happiness

A wise man once wrote, "True happiness begins when the children leave home and the dog dies." Every parent can be certain of two things: (1) the dog is going to stay dead, and (2) the children are coming back. And more often than not, they are bringing somebody with them.

It is important that your children always know that you love them. They came into the world depending on you and they never stop. It makes them feel secure, and it makes you feel important. With this in mind, I have devised methods to handle some problems that eventually come up with your grown children.

Sooner or later, you are going to get a call from your child telling you that for one reason or another, he or she needs to move back home. The reason for the return can be anything from a divorce, to a lost job, to run-of-the-mill money problems.

If you say "no," you are going to feel guilty and never be able to sleep or look in the mirror again. On the other hand, if you say "yes," your empty-nest happiness is going to disappear like quarters in a casino. To say the very least, it is a sticky problem that must be handled with love, understanding, diplomacy, and sneakiness.

With your voice oozing tenderness and compassion, here is what you say: "Sugar, you know that my house is your house. You are my child and you are welcome wherever I am. There is no sacrifice I would not make for you. Whatever I can do to take the potholes out of your road of life, I am willing to do. However, before we start checking rates on U-Haul trucks, let me ask you a couple of questions. What would it take to set you up in your own apartment? How much money would the deposit, rent, and utilities cost your dear old dad? I know that we may have trouble finding a place that allows goats, but let's at least look around."

This plan is foolproof and will allow you to live out your golden years in peace and tranquility. It will also assure you that you will only have to see your in-laws on holidays, and you will never have to stand outside your own bathroom door and listen to them gargle. I don't think anybody over fifty should ever have to listen to their son-in-law or daughter-in-law gargle.

The other phone call you are sure to get from your grown offspring will be a request to allow them to store a "few" things in your garage for about a month. What they are really saying in code is, "Can I fill your tidy, well-arranged garage with enough junk to fill an airplane hangar, and may I leave it there until the day after Jesus comes back?"

Here again, your reply should be filled with phony sincerity. You should say, "Hey! I've got a better idea than that. You don't want to keep your beautiful second-hand furniture in my old garage. Why don't I rent a storage room for you? I don't want you to feel rushed, so I will rent it for three months. Only you will have the key, so you will know it is absolutely safe. I mean, you can't be too careful; after all, K-Mart furniture doesn't grow on trees." This is a plan that works every time, and it will only cost you about a hundred dollars.

In your day-to-day contact with your out-of-the-nest children, let them know that the umbilical cord is still intact and always will be. They should know by your words and deeds that you are not only their parent, but their best friend. Let them know all of that, but

always keep in mind that your biggest oblig-
ation to them is to teach them independence
from you and everybody else. They will never
be happy until they learn one of life's best
rules: If it is to be, it's up to me.

The Home

Leo and Pauline are senior citizens, great Americans, and a little bit nuts. They live in the nude wing of the Memories Are Us Retirement Home.

The nude wing at the home is not necessarily occupied by nudists. It's occupied by old people who, from time to time, like to look at each other naked.

The residents of the nude wing come up with many activities to fill their retirement years. They have a flower show every year. Leo has won twice for best dried arrangement.

The highlight of their summer is their nude skydiving contest. Their announced goal is to fill the Southern skies with naked old people.

Rules for the naked skydiving contest are strict. Contestants must be over eighty years old and a resident of the nude wing of an accredited retirement home. Contestants can only wear a parachute, goggles, and a toe tag that reads "In the event of an accident, return wearer to Memories Are Us Retirement

Home, Forest Park, Georgia."

The amazing thing about the contest is the fact that there have been no confirmed injuries in the seven years the contest has been held. There was one false alarm.

The authorities thought Burt had been killed in 1993. All investigations stopped, however, when an autopsy showed that he had been dead several days when they threw him out of the airplane.

The acknowledged leader of all activities at the home is Luther Phillips. Luther is a regular caller on my show and he keeps us advised of all nude-wing activities. Luther claims to be 104 years old. For the past four years, his sweetheart has been a beautiful young lady known only as Buffy. Buffy just celebrated her twenty-second birthday. Luther is rich, and the gossipmongers at the home think Luther's money is what attracts the nubile Buffy. Luther, however, is convinced that the attraction for Buffy is his superhuman sexual prowess. Luther told me that every Wednesday night, three orderlies take him to Buffy's condo and leave him there overnight. First thing Thursday morning, five orderlies come to bring him back to the home. I asked Luther why it took only three orderlies to deliver him and five to pick him up. His smiling reply was, "I fight 'em."

Leo and Pauline are the only married couple in the nude wing. They are both in their nineties. Pauline is a former beauty queen having been elected "Miss Back Seat" by the 1922 University of Alabama football team.

Leo's claim to fame is that in his long-past youth, he was known as one of the great bank walkers of all time. For those dear readers who were not raised in the South, I should explain that a bank walker is a young man so proud of what Mother Nature has given him that he likes to display himself by walking nude around the bank of the old swimming hole.

Rumor has it that on a recent trip to Panama City, Leo was lost for three days. He was trying to bank walk around the Gulf of Mexico. Details of his walk are sketchy, but Luther told me that there are three outstanding warrants for Leo in the Florida panhandle. The last word we had about Leo and Pauline is that they had a serious argument.

Leo said, "Why don't you ever tell me when you're sexually satisfied?

Pauline said, "Because you're never home."

A Man's
THRONE
is his
CASTLE

Toilets

It has always struck me as strange that in America we are ashamed of our toilets. It bothers us to the point that we won't even say the word. We call them "bathrooms," even if they are in gas stations with no tub or shower and with a sink so filthy no self-respecting alligator would drink from it.

We call them "rest rooms." I have never been able to figure that one out. We call them cute names like the "little boys' room," the "potty," and the "johnny."

In certain sections of the industrialized north, they are called the "can" or the "crapper." In rural America, they are "privies" or "outhouses." In the Army, they are called "latrines"; in the Navy, "heads."

One chain of fast fish restaurants calls them the "necessary rooms." Boy! You can't argue with the logic of that one.

In many restaurants, the management is so embarrassed by the presence of toilets in their establishments, they won't even put "Men" and "Women" on the doors. They insist on cute, cute names like "Cowboys" and "Cowgirls"; "Braves" and "Squaws"; "Pointers" and "Setters"; and for the nature lovers among us, you will find "Bucks" and "Does."

When it comes to toilets in our great country, we simply don't want to admit that we have toilets in our great country. I have given this a lot of thought, and have reached the conclusion that somewhere along the line, we convinced ourselves that it is less than genteel to have a bowel movement.

Have you ever noticed that when you are at a party at someone's home, and you go to their bathroom, if you knock on the door or rattle the handle, anybody in there responds in a loud voice, "Somebody is in here"? We don't even want the person knocking to know who is inside. We seem to be ashamed of this natural, biological act. We should not be bothered by it; almost everybody uses the toilet. I can only think of three exceptions: the Pope, Brenda Starr, and Nancy Reagan.

I have marveled at the many different types of toilets I have been exposed to in my life. I have always been a little puzzled by the two-hole outhouse. Why on God's green Earth would anyone want to sit next to someone else at a time in their day when solitude and a gathering of one's thoughts are so important? What would you talk about?

"Well, Mom, what kind of day did you have?"

"Judy, did you do your homework?"

"Great breakfast, dear. Boy! Am I stuffed."

I can't think of any thoughts that I want to share with anyone during that time in my day.

The old-fashioned outhouse was unfurnished, except for a Sears and Roebuck catalog. The catalog had two uses, and only one of them was reading. The outhouse was as cold as a penguin's knee in the winter, and as hot as the attic of Hades in the summer. During the hot months, there was always a wasp's nest to make sure you did not linger over your catalog.

Almost all outhouses had a half-moon cut into the door. I have never been able to find out why the half-moon symbol was used, unless some guy in Turkey invented the outhouse.

The outhouse has been honored in both song and poem. Old-timers have moist eyes when they speak of the old family privy. If one did not know better, one might think they actually enjoyed using these primitive toilets.

The fact of the matter is the outhouse was barely one step above using the bushes.

Toilets around the world are as different as cotton and cucumbers. The Russians are the only people on our planet who have managed to put an outhouse indoors and make it worse. Their public toilets are all different. They vary from nothing more than a hole in the floor to commodes placed in teeny tiny closets.

The only common denominator seems to be that they are never very clean and none are vented. Therefore, they all smell like what they are. God, I hate it when a toilet smells like a toilet!

The Russian public toilet with the hole in the floor has the outline of two footprints marked on either side of the hole. I guess the theory is that if you stand on the footprints, you are in the correct position to line up with the hole. It only takes one trip to realize that their calculations in this respect are greatly flawed. Every time I went into a Russian toilet, it became obvious to me that the previous occupant didn't know anything about standing in footprints.

In private Russian homes, the toilets are only slightly better than their public counterparts.

It is a little bitty unvented closet, in which they have installed a simulated commode. If your legs are not too long, there is a slight chance you can close the door. The toilet paper has the texture of an oak leaf. Mr. Whipple would be in serious trouble in the Kremlin. I am convinced that if he squeezed Russian toilet paper, he would be in grave danger of hurting his hand. It is so coarse that in some hotels there are signs advising you not to flush the paper. I'm proud to say that one of my biggest blows to communism was to ignore those signs.

Russian ballet dancers are acclaimed worldwide for their excellence. My theory is that after a lifetime of using Russian toilet paper, walking on your toes becomes very natural.

For some reason known only to Russians, their commodes do not come with lids on them. It is possible to buy a piece of cloth-covered cardboard to use as a lid. You find these, however, in only the finer Russian toilets.

Due to the tiny size of their toilets, it is impossible to throw up with the door closed. It is hard enough to maintain your dignity while throwing up without everyone within earshot stopping by to pay their respects in broken English.

When I was a small child, one of the great joys of my young life was riding the train. The bathrooms on American trains in those days were a great adventure. I was a child who was easily amused, so flushing the toilet held great interest for me. I was amazed that you could look down into the commode and see the roadbed speeding by. There was always a sign that read "Passengers will please refrain from flushing toilets while the train is standing in the station." This made perfect sense to me and I never disobeyed; besides, it couldn't be much fun to flush a commode on a train that was not moving.

Russian trains are vastly different from our trains. They have no dining car, no baggage car, and no club car. They are meant to get you from point A to point B without wasting time on your comfort or well-being. I have only made two trips on Russian trains; one lasted nine hours, the other fourteen hours. When Mother Nature summoned me, I thought, "Hey! I'm going to get to see a Russian roadbed." I got up and went looking for the toilet. I found it, opened the door, and the smell was like every goat in the world had preceded me into this green-haze-filled horror. The door was no more than half-opened when every orifice in my body slammed shut.

Whatever urge had brought me to the thresh-
old of that room was instantly gone, and gone
permanently. I was never able to step inside a
Russian train's toilet, and to this day, have never
seen a Russian roadbed.

The U.S. military has many unique and
unusual toilet customs. To start with, they,
like the rest of the world, will not call them
what they are. I was in the Marine Corps where
they were known as "heads" or simply "The
Head." (I have never checked, but I'd bet a bun-
dle that the origin of that would boggle the
mind.) In the average Marine Corps head, there
are about fifteen commodes. They are sepa-
rated by wooden partitions. However, they have
no doors. The commodes and their com-
partments are identical, except for one. The
lone exception is always on the end and is
marked by a sign that reads "V.D. only."
The V.D.-only commode is always the clean-
est one in the head. Nobody ever uses it, or
for that matter, walks very close to it.

When we were in the field, we were con-
stantly digging what they called "latrines."
"Latrine" is a French word that I think means
"deep hole in the ground where Marines pee."
There is also a thing they called the "slit trench"

which is a dehumanizing thing to use.

The most interesting place to relieve yourself was nameless as far as I know. First, you dug a long ditch. It was usually about fifteen feet long and five feet deep. Into the ditch, you poured about one foot of government-issue gravel or sand. Then you stood a pipe on end in the ditch; the other end of the pipe was now sticking about three or three and a half feet above the ground. The next step was to fill the ditch with dirt. Then funnels were attached to the top of the pipe, and when you took a whiz, you did it into the funnel. I never understood why my government would involve me in this project. I guess it was just the military way, but I always felt like it really played hell with the water table.

No matter how many man-hours we spent digging latrines, slit trenches, or that funnel thing, we always marched off in a day or so and left them there. Silent testimony that the Marines had been there and that the situation had been well in hand.

The newest craze in toilet technology can be found in fancy hotels and new office buildings. The urinals are equipped with what they call a "magic eye." When you walk away from it, the urinal flushes automatically. Call me old-fashioned, but when I'm standing in front of a urinal, I don't want any eye on me, magic or otherwise.

While airplane toilets are small, they can be either very clean or very messy, depending on the amount of turbulence. Once, on a bumpy flight from Atlanta to Houston, I was next in line for the toilet behind a man who had been drinking beer after beer since we took off. When it was my turn, I found that every surface—floor, walls, and ceiling—was soaked. The water in the commode, however, was springlike in its purity.

Pay toilets have pretty much passed from the scene. I think most folks think it is taking capitalism too far to charge an American for going to the toilet.

When my daughter, Barbara, was about three years old, she set forth to see and use every service station bathroom in America. This fascinated her. Her favorite line to get me to stop the car was to say, "Daddy, I've got to go NOW!" Before I would take her to the door, she would always ask the question, "Is it decent?" In her three-year-old wisdom, she had discovered the only important question about a toilet . . . Is it decent?

Sentimental JOURNEYS

Co-Cola

It has become popular in the last few years to refer to everything as America's own, like "America's Team," "America's Truck," and "America's Network."

I have had a love affair all my life with America's soft drink, Coca-Cola (pronounced in the Deep South as Co-Cola). It was as much a part of my youth as red clay, marbles, or Dagwood Bumstead.

When I was five or six years old, Coca-Cola was the ultimate treat; six ounces of Heaven for only a nickel. It came in a bottle shaped a little like an hourglass. When you reached down into the murky, ice-cold water of Johnny Durham's drink box, you could always find the Coke by that wonderful bottle's shape.

There were other soft drinks on the market, and most all of them gave you more for a nickel than did my beloved Coke. I must confess that several times on a real hot, humid Georgia day, I would find myself in a backsliding condition and go for the bigger size of a Pepsi or an RC. I might even go for a Red Rock Cola or a Red Rock Ginger Ale. If my taste called for a fruit flavor, I would get an orange Crush, or a grape NeHi, or even a strawberry-flavored Town Hall. These experiments were short-lived, I'm proud to say, because I always came back to "the pause that refreshes."

When World War II came along, Coke was one of the first things to become in short supply. In my six-year-old mind, I couldn't figure out how our soldiers and sailors were using Coca-Cola to whip the Germans and the Japanese. When I asked a grown-up, he said the army needed the sugar. That didn't make any sense to me, but I guess it was true because we won the war and got our Cokes back.

In my teen years, Coke became an even bigger part of my life. I'm not sure at what age a boy's hormones kick in and his mind turns from baseball, basketball, and football to girls, and girls, and girls. I'm not sure when it happens, but I do remember all the signs of the ballistic hormones. There are ten sure signs:

1. You stop going barefooted.
2. Your haircut is suddenly important.
3. You shine your shoes without being told.

4. You try aftershave lotion even if you don't shave.

5. For the first time in your life, the telephone becomes important.

6. Your mother can never iron your shirt just right.

7. It is out of the question to wear a patch on your jeans.

8. You stop spitting.

9. You experiment to see if indeed "a little dab will do you."

10. You worry a lot about how tall you are.

It is at about this time when you introduce some new lines into your speech: "What are you doing after school?" "Want to stop by Glover's Pharmacy for a cherry Coke?" "Come on, I'll buy you a Coke."

I wonder how many teenage romances started out over a fountain Coke. The setting was not always the same, but from border to border and coast to coast, it looked something very much like this:

A teenage boy and girl sit at a soda fountain. The table is simulated marble; the chairs are wrought iron. On the table are two small fountain Cokes with a single paper straw in each glass. A ceiling fan spins slowly and silently overhead. Behind the counter stands the soda jerk wearing a starched Ike jacket, a white apron, and sometimes a black bow tie. All that atmosphere and it only costs a dime.

In addition to the flowering of young romance over two small Cokes, our teen years are filled with Coca-Cola. Shake a Coke with your thumb over the top and spray somebody. This is an all-purpose celebration or an all-purpose prank which can lead to a great deal of laughter or a punch in the mouth, depending on the sense of humor of the sprayee.

The ultimate snack is a handful of peanuts poured right into your bottle of Coke. It's tasty enough to make your eyes roll back in your head.

A Coke dessert? How about a scoop of vanilla ice cream into a big glass of that Heavenly liquid; easy to make and fun to eat. It's called a Coke float.

Did you ever make Coca-Cola ice cream? It ain't peach, but it's wonderful.

Whenever I hear about Cola wars, I have to smile. Coke not only tastes best, but it is so entwined with our country's history that it will always be number one by a mile.

When Henry Ford was still running a bicycle shop, Americans were enjoying Coca-Cola. When the doughboys came home from the trenches of France, they wanted hamburgers and Cokes. Ask any World War II veteran how much he missed Coke. Co-Cola is as American as the flag.

My beautiful wife, Diane, summed it up best when she took a drink of Coke and said, "The taste of Coke is like the smell of bacon frying."

Gone but Not Forgotten

Time is a magician. I say that because time, for no good reason, can make things disappear. Sometimes they disappear almost overnight, like the Edsel; other things take years to vanish, like pocket watches.

That was the way it was with telephone booths. It seems like only yesterday phone booths were like a little home away from home. They were equipped with folding doors that closed to keep noise out and your secret conversation in. There was a small fan with rubber blades to keep you cool and a small seat so you could be comfy while you chatted away. The cost for all this luxury was five cents per call. Cool, comfortable, private, and it only cost a nickel!

You can say what you will about kryptonite's being Superman's worst enemy, but take away that old-fashioned phone booth, and all that's left of the man of steel is a funny looking guy in a suit and horn-rimmed glasses, looking for a place to change clothes.

When did women stop wearing hats and gloves? It seems to me that only yesterday, when you went downtown or to church or rode on an airplane, all of the women wore hats and gloves. Who decided that was no longer the thing to do?

What happened to those wonderful caps that nurses wore? They not only looked sharp, they were a badge of education, honor, dedication, and a silent pledge to fight human suffering wherever they found it. I wonder how many little girls decided to dedicate their lives to nursing because those caps were so striking. Who decided to throw them all away?

I wonder who the hero was who decided we didn't need vent windows in our cars anymore. I betcha he was the same yahoo who decided you didn't need a spare tire, because you could get by with an oversized doughnut in your trunk. Could he have been the one who got rid of the rumble seat and the running boards, and moved the dimmer switch off of the floorboard? I don't know who he was, but a good caning seems to be in order if we ever find out.

What happened to gas station attendants? It was a great comfort to pull up to a gas pump, run over that rubber hose, hear the bell ring, and just sit there. In about fifteen seconds, Marvin would come out of one of the bays (you knew his name was Marvin because it was sewn over his pocket). He was always wiping his hands off on a rag. His greeting was the same to every customer, "Can I hep you?"

Whatever happened to him? God, how I loved old Marvin. It wouldn't be so bad, except that Marvin has been replaced by an unsmiling guy with no name on his shirt. Mr. No Name sits inside a glass cage. He speaks to you in fractured English through an intercom that is carefully programmed to pick up every fourth word. The worst part is Mr. No Name doesn't even have the simple human decency to wipe his hands on a rag. No sense of tradition whatsoever. Goodbye Marvin; America misses you.

Whatever happened to *The Saturday Evening Post?* I miss "Hazel," "The Perfect Squelch," and those wonderful Norman Rockwell covers.

I miss the old steam whistles on trains. The whistles on the diesel engines sound like an angry rhino passing gas.

I miss playing in old, abandoned sawdust piles (they don't allow grown-ups to do that).

I miss hide-and-seek (something else grown-ups can't do).

I miss Bing Crosby at Christmas time.

Sometimes it seems like I am a stranger on my own planet, or perhaps I'm not on my own planet. The one I came from had Roosevelt, Truman, and Ike. It had penny loafers, poodle skirts, and John Wayne. It had kitchen matches, Henry J. automobiles, and the Brooklyn Dodgers.

Common sense tells me that, in the end, the calendar will always win, and in my heart I know that we live in a better world—a world without polio, Hitler, or the black plague. Yes, sir, all things considered, it is a better world, but I'm still a little worried about old Marvin.

Good Neighbors

From time to time on my radio show, I do a feature called "Neighbors from Hell." The premise is simple: call me on the radio and tell me about your bad neighbors. You learn quickly that the world is indeed full of neighbors better suited to the underworld.

You hear about neighbors who have drunken parties, are involved in shootings, or play loud music from midnight till 4:00 a.m. You hear about the neighbors who keep broken, major appliances on the front porch. You hear from suspicious callers who suspect their neighbors of being everything from whorehouse madams to dope dealers.

One caller was convinced that her neighbor was a German spy. I explained to her that the war with Germany had been over for almost fifty years. It did not change her mind.

If you talk to enough people about their bad neighbors, it will make you want to live on a boat. With the universe abounding with such bad neighbors, I have set forth on a mental journey to find the world's best neighbor. These are the people I would actually like to live next to:

FIBBER AND MOLLY McGEE

The McGees lived at 79 Wistful Vista in the town of Wistful Vista. It must have been a wonderful town, because nobody seemed to work too hard. Fibber and Molly mostly stayed home and waited for visitors to drop by. On any given day, their guests might include Mayor LaTrivia, the Great Gildersleeve, and the Old-Timer. They were all interesting, funny people, and I would have enjoyed sharing some of Molly's coffee with them in the McGee living room.

BLONDIE AND DAGWOOD BUMSTEAD

I don't know exactly where the Bumsteads lived, but it was a nice middle-class neighborhood. Blondie would be a perfect neighbor, and Dagwood probably wouldn't be any problem since he wanted to spend most of his off time napping. Their kids were perfect, and their dog, Daisy, would never use your front lawn for a bathroom. In almost sixty years in the funny papers, there is not one mention of Daisy having a bowel movement. My kind of dog.

THE INVISIBLE MAN

I would love to have the Invisible Man for a neighbor, because I wouldn't care what he did as long as he was quiet about it.

BOB AND JOANNA HARTLEY

Bob and Joanna owned and operated the lovely Stratford Inn on TV's "Newhart." Located in snowy Vermont, the Stratford Inn would be one of my favorite places to live. It was beautiful and the neighbors were more than interesting. It would be a laugh a second to hang out not only with Bob and Joanna, but with their handyman, George Utley. George was a second-generation handyman at the Stratford Inn. He was friendly, funny, and would definitely make a world-class neighbor. Not only that, but you could borrow all the tools you would ever need from good old George.

Stephanie was the maid at the inn. She was a spoiled, stuck-up rich girl. She never thought about anybody except herself. The only thing that would make her a good neighbor was the fact that it was fun to watch her walk.

Then there were the three brothers, Larry, Darryl, and Darryl. They made the three stooges look like members of the Joint Chiefs. They owned a business called Anything for a Buck. They never shaved, bathed, or combed their hair. Two of them never even spoke. They did, however, show a great love for each other and for mankind in general. Everything they did was either loving or stupid. You can't ask much more than that from a neighbor.

LUCY AND RICKY RICARDO

Wouldn't it be great fun to sit down for dinner at night and have your wife tell you what she saw that "crazy redhead" do today? The only real downside with Ricky next door would be the bongos after 9:00 p.m.

MARY RICHARDS, FROM
"THE MARY TYLER MOORE SHOW"

If Mary Richards was your next-door neighbor, you could fill your spare time waiting for her friends to drop by. Lou, Ted, and Murray were part of one of the best sitcoms ever made.

The people listed in this chapter would all come high on my list of desirable neighbors. None of them, however, would be my number one choice. If I could pick any neighbor in the world, it would be:

SHERIFF ANDY TAYLOR

Can you imagine how interesting life could be

in Mayberry, North Carolina, living next door
to Andy, Opie, and Aunt Bea? Think about
your typical Sunday. It would start with Sunday school and service at All Souls' Church. If
you were lucky you might even have Andy as
your Sunday school teacher.

At church you would hear a lot of your
friends singing in the choir. Andy and Aunt Bea,
Gomer and Barney, as well as Helen Crump and
Thelma Lou.

After dinner you could relax on Andy's front
porch and enjoy the fine weather. It was usually seventy-two degrees in Mayberry, year-
round. There was never any talk of politics or
anything else that could evolve into unpleas-
antness. No business whatsoever was con-
ducted in Mayberry on Sundays. But, when the
sun came up on Monday, this wonderful town
sprang back to life, and everybody got back to
making a living.

Andy and Barney were at the courthouse.
Helen was at school, and Floyd Lawson was
busy cutting hair and quoting Calvin Coolidge.
Gomer was at Wally's service station explain-
ing to new customers that there was no charge
for air and water, but they did charge for gas
and oil.

Juanita was at the diner, and Clara Edwards

was getting ready to teach piano to Mayberry's children. Otis Campbell was nursing his usual Monday-morning hangover on the job at the furniture plant as a glue dipper. Aunt Bea was busy cleaning house and preparing lunch for Andy and Barney and any prisoners who might be at the jail. Mayor Stoner was shuffling papers and trying to think of some way to irritate the sheriff. Thelma Lou was at her desk, and Howard Sprague was fulfilling his duties as city clerk.

At first glance, you might think that there was not much to do in Mayberry. No major league football, baseball, or basketball. No bowling alley or even cable TV. The chief source of entertainment was visiting. The citizens of Mayberry enjoyed each other's company and good old-fashioned conversation. I think, deep down inside, everybody would like to have Andy Taylor of Mayberry as his next-door neighbor.

Riding the Iron Rails

At the moment of this writing, debate echoes around the halls of Congress about national health care. There are people in high places who think the government can look after our health care. It seems that anytime our society faces a big problem those affected shout in a loud voice, "Somebody ought to pass a law. The government should do something." Well, a while back the government did do something. Let me tell you a little story.

A few years ago, passenger train service was in trouble in America. The railroads were losing money in a big, big way, so the government came up with Amtrak. The government was going to run our passenger trains.

Like most people, I don't get to ride trains as much as I once did. The pressures of my business force me to fly almost everywhere I go. However, I have very fond memories of rail travel. I was, therefore, tickled nearly to death when, a few years ago, I had the opportunity to make a round trip by train from Atlanta to New Orleans. I had wonderful memories of the old Southern Crescent taking me to New Orleans, and I looked forward to doing it all again.

We got on the train at 7:30 a.m. The first thing I noticed as wrong was the conductor. The uniform was okay, but the hat was out of kilter. It was not a real, honest-to-God conductor's hat. It looked like something a World War II pilot would wear. Also, the conductor did not have gray hair. Thinking back to the good old days of train travel, I could not remember ever seeing a real conductor who did not have gray hair. How in the name of Casey Jones could you expect a conductor to conduct with that funny hat and no gray hair? I was so enthusiastic about the trip, however, that I decided to overlook this government lackey's weak impression of a real conductor.

Inside the train was mass confusion. The passengers did not know where to sit, and the government workers assigned to take care of such things were milling around as confused as a herd of sheep. After about forty-five minutes and a few minor miracles that I can only attribute to Divine intervention, we all found our assigned seats. My stomach told me that it was time for breakfast, so we made our way to the dining car.

The dining car was not the way I remembered it, either. The snow-white tablecloths were gone. The vase with the single fresh flower was gone. And, dear Lord, say it ain't so, those wonderful dining-car waiters with their crisp, clean, white jackets were gone.

The tables and chairs had been replaced with plastic, modular booths that had obviously been purchased at a Burger Doodle going-out-of-business sale. They were uncomfortable, they were too small for any adult human, and they were ugly. No tablecloth, no vase, and no fresh flower.

The dining car was packed for breakfast. The government had managed to find two women who were obviously former Nazi prison-camp guards and tried to pass them off as waitresses. They barely passed as Earthlings. It seemed to take forever, but finally one of them came to our table and said in a flat, cold voice, "Are you people ready?"

I said, "Do you serve grits?"

She said, "Do you see them on the menu?"

"We haven't seen a menu," I said.

She gestured toward a four-by-four plastic card in a plastic holder sitting on the table. Then she snarled, "I'll be back when you've written down your order."

We checked the very limited menu and finally wrote down our order on the pads that the Nazi lady had provided. Our breakfast was served in square Styrofoam plates. The coffee was served in Styrofoam cups. The utensils were plastic. The juice came in plastic cups with aluminum foil glued to the top. It was not the worst food I've ever had, but I felt then and I feel now that it would have caused a riot if it had been served to the inmates of Devil's Island.

The waitresses were scurrying up and down the aisles, and on one occasion, one of them bumped into my knee. She said in a loud voice, "You're gonna have to keep your knee out of the aisle, fella." I thought that must be the way they teach government workers to say, "Excuse me."

When breakfast was over, we made our way back to our seats. I read for a few minutes, and then lay my head back on the seat and closed my eyes. The only sound that I was aware of was the clickety-clack of the rails. It came to me suddenly that the only thing remaining of the old Southern Crescent was the clickety-clack of the rails. As I sat there, my mind rushed back to the day before government "saved" our rail travel.

I remembered another trip I had taken on the

Southern Crescent. My bags were carried on board by a smiling man wearing a bright red cap. He checked my ticket and took me to the car. He told me what seat I was to sit in, and as I was getting on board, he said, "I hope you have a safe trip and I'll look forward to seeing you when you get back to Atlanta."

I passed the gray-haired conductor who smiled and said, "Good morning, nice to have you with us." We pulled out of the station right on time.

Nobody announced that it was time for breakfast. You knew it because the aroma of biscuits, ham, and bacon made its way through the length of the train. I was met at the door of the dining car by the dining-car steward, a well-groomed man in his middle to late thirties. Smiling, he said, "Two for breakfast? Yes, sir, right this way."

The dining car was furnished like a fine restaurant. Wooden tables with high-back chairs, and lots of room between tables so you never felt crowded. Our table was covered with a snow-white tablecloth. There were silver salt and pepper shakers, a vase with a single carnation, and silver knives, forks, and spoons. There was a cup and saucer. Written in small, proud, red letters on each piece of china were the words "Southern Railway."

Our waiter was at the table only seconds after we sat down. He was a tall, distinguished black man carrying a silver coffee pot with a very ornate "S" engraved on it.

He was smiling as he poured our coffee. He handed us a two-page breakfast menu and said, "Mr. Porch, (he had taken the time to know my name), I'll be right back to get your order and answer any questions you have."

I had ham, eggs, and yes, praise be to Robert E. Lee, they brought me grits and I didn't even have to ask. When I was about one-third of the way through my breakfast, our waiter stopped by the table and said, "Mr. Porch, those eggs look a little too done."

I said, "No, they're just fine."

"Are you sure?" he said, "I'll be glad to get you some more if they're not just the way you like 'em."

While he was at our table, he poured us some more hot coffee. When he brought us the Atlanta morning paper he said, "Thought you might want to see what's going on in Atlanta while you're out of town."

In the middle of the afternoon, we went to the club car to have a drink. We sat down on a large, comfortable sofa, and within seconds a waiter arrived to take our order. He repeated the same fine service we had enjoyed at breakfast.

When we got off the train that night in New Orleans, we felt like we had been traveling with friends. We were not tired because the wonderful folks on the Southern Crescent had worked very hard to see that our trip had been a fun, relaxing experience. They took pride in their jobs. They were good at what they did, and it was apparent that they enjoyed it.

The defenders of Amtrak say that if the government had not stepped in, there would be no more rail travel in this country. I take a different view. I think the Southern Crescent should have been treated like an old, dear friend and allowed to die with her dignity intact, not taken over by a crowd of government workers who not only don't know how to run a railroad, but have no desire to learn.

Rail travel did not die in America; it was murdered. And the thing that hurts most is they used our tax dollars to pay for the killing.

Government-run health care? That's really going to be something!

Prison Movies, or "This Cracker Box Can't Hold Rocky"

Movies seem to go in cycles. In the 1930s and 1940s, Hollywood was turning out an average of two motion pictures a day. Love stories, Westerns, musicals, and one of my favorites, the prison movie.

If anybody has made a good, old-fashioned prison movie in the last few decades, I don't know about it. I had great hopes for *Cool Hand Luke.* It turned out not to be a prison movie at all. It was a chain gang movie. Prison movies are filmed almost entirely indoors, and chain gang movies are filmed almost entirely outdoors. Chain gang movies are always set in the South with a lot of swamps for the inmates to work in. They have sadistic guards named Floyd or Rufus to abuse the convicts. Prison movies are usually set up north and the guards are all named Slade or Kincaid.

The jury is still out on why Hollywood no longer makes prison movies. I think there is a market for them. The formula is simple enough. You do exactly what movie makers did in the 1940s and 1950s.

The warden can be a good guy or a bad guy. If he is a good guy, he can be played by Pat O'Brien. If he is a bad guy, he can be played by Barton McLain.

The hero/convict can be a good guy who got framed or a louse who deserves everything he gets. If he is a good guy who got framed, he can be played by Joel McRae or Douglas Fairbanks Jr. If he is a louse who deserves everything he gets, he can be played by James Cagney, Edward G. Robinson, or George Raft.

If he is a good guy who got framed, his name must be Steve. If he is a louse who deserves everything he gets, his name must be Rocky.

His girlfriend must be played by Sylvia Sydney or Clair Trevor. If Steve escapes from prison, it must be in order to prove his innocence. On the other hand, if Rocky (the louse) escapes, it is to resume his life of crime and to beat up Clair Trevor or Sylvia Sydney on occasion.

Any self-respecting prison movie must have at least one scene showing a convict being led to the electric chair by two guards, the warden, and a priest. The priest has to be reading the Bible as they walk toward the chair. I have done extensive research and determined that no protestants were ever executed in a prison movie.

When the louse is led out of his cell and starts his slow walk to the chair, several things must be happening:

- The priest must be looking at his Bible and muttering in a low voice with an Irish accent.

- The hallway leading to the chair must be lit by a series of forty-watt bulbs.

- One of the men on death row must be black, have a bass voice, and be singing "Swing Low Sweet Chariot." It is of paramount importance that he be a bass. (A tenor would probably invoke laughter from the priest and ruin the somber mood.)

- The louse must shake hands with the priest and say, "So long, Fodder." In the better prison movies, all condemned men are from New York City.

- Executions should only take place on stormy nights.

- The prison lights should dim so the audience will know that justice has been served, and the black guy can stop singing, and the priest can stop muttering.

I don't guess they will ever make another real prison movie, but if they do, I'm available as director and technical advisor.

Love

I think the most misunderstood thing in the world is love. Love is different for everybody. Poets and songwriters have been trying for years without success to tell us what love is and how it works. One songwriter put pen to paper and came up with "You always hurt the one you love." That's dumb on the face of it. Sometimes you hurt folks you don't give a rip about.

It all boils down to one simple fact: love means different things to different people.

Love is sitting up all night in a hospital waiting room.

Love is watching her sleep.

Love is the feeling you get watching your son get his first haircut.

Love is bringing her flowers when it's not a special occasion.

Love is when you enjoy her beating you at Scrabble.

Love is when she fixes your favorite meal and she is as tired as you are.

Love is the smell of baby powder.

Love is when she walks by your chair and touches the top of your head.

Love is the thing that makes you hum.

Love is the basis of religion, patriotism, and all success. Love is the only thing that can make you deliriously happy and miserably sad at the same time.

Love does not mean never having to say you're sorry. Love means being able to say you're sorry and really, really mean it. Love is simply the most important thing in the world.

PORCH
Potpourri

Never milk a cow with one udder, unless you want a friend for life.

✣ ✣ ✣

The meek shall inherit the earth . . . if the rest of you folks don't mind.

✣ ✣ ✣

A Third World Country is any country where you can't buy sweet iced tea.

Bombproof Outhouse

Being a grown-up is not as much fun as I
thought it would be.

❖ ✛ ❖

Ignorance is like concrete . . . the longer it
stays, the tougher it is to get rid of.

❖ ✛ ❖

Arizona is the place where people go to die
and don't.

Toulouse-Laurabbit

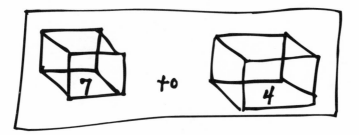

Box Scores

**Most insects should not
wear polka dots.**

History will show that Hillary Clinton was never called the "First Chick."

✛ ✛ ✛

Speak with love and kindness to quiet thy brother's wrath. That failing, knock his lights out.

✛ ✛ ✛

A drunk employee is a happy employee.

Nobody seemed to remember how Horny Johnson got his nickname.

Porch Potpourri

I am harassed by the way Dolly Parton
breathes.

✛ ✛ ✛

Naval historians now feel the screen doors
on early submarines were a mistake.

✛ ✛ ✛

It is better to have loved and lost than to
have pulled a groin muscle.

QUIZ OF THE DAY:

**Name this famous
character from history.**

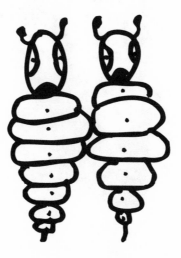

Siamese Bugs

**Only known picture of
Abe Lincoln's sister, Shirley.**

Historians now feel that too much coffee may have made John Wilkes Booth cranky.

✣ ✦ ✣

If you have a home where the buffalo roam, chances are the Health Department is going to drop on you like a load of cordwood.

✣ ✦ ✣

Grease is our friend.

The Woody Allen rat.

Fred was later sorry that he
insulted the witch doctor.

SADDEST SONG EVER WRITTEN:

My mother died on Christmas Day
Holding my little brother,
Who was crippled and
Getting a divorce at the time.

**Beautiful Beautiful
Brown Eye
I'll Never Love Blue Eyes Again**

Riddle: What goes clop, clop, clop, clop, bang, bang, clop, clop?

Answer: an Amish drive-by shooting.

✣ ✣ ✣

Riddle: What goes mmmmmm I keep a close watch on this heart of mine.
I keep my eyes wide open all the time. Bang, bang, mmmmm?

Answer: a drive-by Johnny Cashing.

The clues indicated to O'Mally that he
was looking for a serial killer.

Only a complete fool would buy a battery from a rabbit playing a bass drum and wearing flip-flops.

❖ ✛ ❖

Never date a girl who has a fungus named after her.

❖ ✛ ❖

Radio engineers do it 'til their mega hurts.

**In the early days, T.V. sets
used real rabbit ears.**

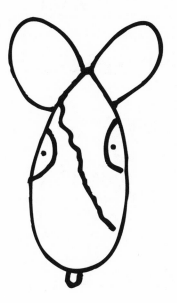

Scarface Al Carabbit

**Only known picture of
King Leon, the Loud.**

In the language of the Apache, *Arizona* means "why don't they air-condition this mother?"

❖ ✛ ❖

Lizzie Borden took an axe and gave her mother forty whacks.
When she saw what she had done, she gave her father forty-one . . . thus becoming eligible for the orphans' picnic.

❖ ✛ ❖

January 9th is the best day to get a haircut and drown your nephew.

Pee Wee Herman taking a
break at the movies.

Pee Wee Herman's new theme song: "It Had To Be Me."

✣ ✢ ✣

Only poor people think that money won't buy happiness.

✣ ✢ ✣

Any problem can be solved if the proper amount of violence is used.

I thought I would drop you a note.

The Oregon Trail was more than real estate, it was where Hoppy and Gabby first fell in love.

✤ ✤ ✤

In the language of the Apache, there is no word for *Motorola.*

✤ ✤ ✤

Question: What do you get when you cross Lassie with a pit bull?

Answer: You get a dog that will tear your leg off and then go for help.

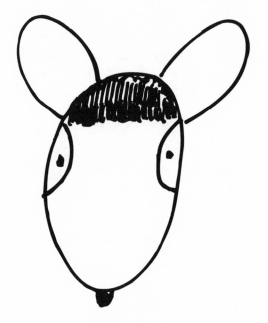

Mamie Eisenrat

SONG LYRICS THAT DIDN'T QUITE MAKE IT:

✤ ✚ ✤

"If you were the only girl in the world,
I'd try to get there early . . ."

"The green, green controlled substance
of home . . ."

"Ain't no sunshine when she's here . . ."

This is either the only known
picture of a flying saucer
or Pinky Lee's hat.

Question: What happened to the woman who didn't know the difference between Vaseline and putty?

Answer: All her window panes fell out.

❖ ✢ ❖

You load sixteen tons and what do you get? Another day older and dead on your ass.

The Apache warrior was delighted
to have the great honor of scalping
Marlo Thomas.

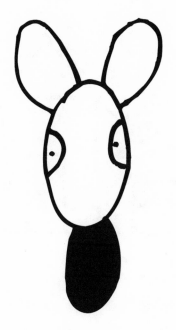

Jimmy Durabbit

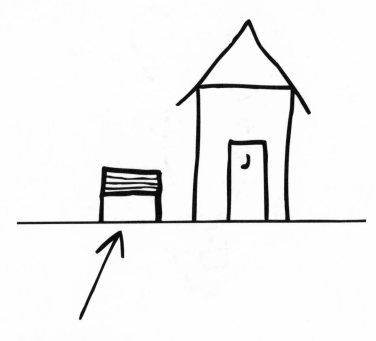

Johnny Bench

My new favorite Country/Western
song titles:

✥ ✚ ✥

"She Left Me Flat in Our Roll-
away Bed"

"Take Your Tongue out of My Mouth,
I'm Kissing You Goodbye"

"If Fingerprints Showed Up on Skin,
Whose Would I Find on You?"

"When They Find Jimmy Hoffa, Then
I'll Come Back to You"

The real Miss Universe contest.

"Superman is indeed faster than a speeding bullet." — Lois Lane, 1976

✠ ✠ ✠

New Red Cross slogan: "Please give blood or we'll take it."

✠ ✠ ✠

Dracula talking to his children: "Don't make me get out of this coffin!"

The photographs in
Pee Wee Herman's locket.

Pee Wee Herman can always get a date on short notice.

✢ ✛ ✢

In the language of the Sioux, there is no word for *Veg-a-matic*.

✢ ✛ ✢

Gun and knife show slogan: "Over 2,000 ways to kill and maim your fellow man."

MANNA
37 FLAVORS
FLAVOR of The MoNTh
BANANA MANNA

**First sign you see when you
get to Heaven.**

PUNCH LINE HALL OF FAME:

✠ ✠ ✠

" . . . and the midget said 'Either the
milk crate is too low or her ears
are on backwards!'"

" . . . Step-ladder, Hell! Bring me a
grape NeHi!'"

" . . . What do you think this is, a duck?'"

Siamese Lollypops

And the Lord spaketh to the people and He said, "Y'all hush."

✥ ✦ ✥

"They always call him Mr. Football . . ."
(Song written about the late sawmill owner
J. Lawrence Football)

Der Feurat

Rin Tin Tin was an egg sucker.

✛ ✛ ✛

The Indians call it Maize. We call it Oprah.

✛ ✛ ✛

"Lincoln is really starting to frost me."
— John Wilkes Booth, 1865

**Nobody seemed to remember how
Hopalong Cassidy got his nickname.**

In the history of the Old West, no cowboy ever named his horse Russell.

❖ ✛ ❖

LITTLE-KNOWN FACTS:
Andy and Barney never beat Aunt Bea with nightsticks. They did, however, give Otis Campbell a Pepsi-Cola enema on June 8, 1966.

❖ ✛ ❖

MAKE UP YOUR OWN JOKE:
" . . . and the midget said, 'Give me the money or I'll jump!'"

**Count Dracula was pleased to
be a Red Cross volunteer.**

MORE OF
MY FAVORITE COUNTRY/WESTERN
SONG TITLES:

❖ ✚ ❖

"Lord, Preserve Us and Protect Us. We've
Been Drinkin' Whiskey Since Breakfast"

"Kiss Me, Hug Me, Make Me
Write Bad Checks"

"Kissing You Makes My Eyes Cross"

"Mama Could Bench Press Loretta Lynn"

**Be my Valentine
or I'll hang your dog.**